Rogue One, a Star wars story :
2017

wind

W9-DBO-060

ᴑᴠᴎᴜᴀᴄᴠᴉ

THE TIDE TURNS

The rebels have won their first victory against the evil Galactic Empire.
The hard–won plans for the Death Star are being rushed to Obi-Wan
Kenobi aboard the *Tantive IV*. As it flees the devastation of the battle of
Scarif and the might of Darth Vader, who is in hot pursuit of Princess Leia
and the brave soldiers of the Rebellion, there is finally the brief opportunity
to reflect on this epic chapter of *Star Wars* lore.

This Mission Debrief covers the heroes, villains, and technology of
Rogue One, with interviews with the cast and crew, and amazing trivia
about the movie.

TITAN EDITORIAL
Editor Jonathan Wilkins
Senior Executive Editor Divinia Fleary
Art Editor Andrew Leung
Designer Russel Seal
Art Director Oz Browne
Sub Editor Neil Edwards
Editorial Assistant Tolly Maggs
Senior Production Controller Jackie
Flook
Production Controller Peter James
Production Supervisor Maria Pearson

Senior Sales Manager Steve Tothill
Subscriptions Executive Tony Ho
Direct Sales & Marketing Manager
Ricky Claydon
Brand Manager, Marketing Lucy Ripper
Commercial Manager Michelle Fairlamb
U.S. Advertising Manager Jeni Smith
Publishing Manager Darryl Tothill
Publishing Director Chris Teather
Operations Director Leigh Baulch
Executive Director Vivian Cheung
Publisher Nick Landau

LUCASFILM EDITORIAL
Senior Editor Brett Rector
Assistant Editor Samantha Holland
Story Group Pablo Hidalgo, Leland
Chee, Matt Martin, Jane Knoll
Image Archives Newell Todd,
Gabrielle Levenson, Erik Sanchez,
Bryce Pinkos, Tim Mapp
Art Director Troy Alders

DISTRIBUTION
US Newsstand: Total Publisher Services, Inc.
John Dziewiatkowski, 630-851-7683
US Distribution: Source Interlink, Curtis Circulation Company
UK Newsstand: Comag, 01895 444 055
US/UK Direct Sales Market: Diamond
Comic Distributors

For more info on advertising contact
adinfo@titanemail.com

Rogue One: Mission Debrief is published by Titan
Magazines, a division of Titan Publishing Group
Limited, 144 Southwark Street, London SE1 0UP.

For sale in the U.S., Canada, U.K. and Eire

ISBN: 9781785861574

CONTENTS

ᔑᔑ⊣ᔑ ⊡⊣ᔑᔑ

R O G U E   O N E
O R I G I N S

The *Rogue One* team takes us
behind the scenes of the movie.

1 /

2 /

The exciting series of stand-alone *Star Wars* stories ushers in a new era for Lucasfilm that will not only deepen and expand the universe but also provide a creative filmmaking platform.

It is particularly fitting that the idea for this series of stories came from George Lucas. When Lucasfilm president and *Star Wars* producer Kathleen Kennedy first sat down with Lucas, he outlined his plans to continue with the *Star Wars* saga and to make Episodes VII, VIII, and IX. Then he revealed another ambition. "George was excited not only about doing more saga films, but also about the potential of doing stand-alone stories that lived and breathed inside the *Star Wars* universe," explains producer Kathleen Kennedy.

"The *Star Wars* episodes (I–VII) follow the Skywalker family and tell a continuing story. The stand-alone movies, which can occur anyplace on the timeline, will introduce new characters and explore a wide variety of genres," Kennedy adds.

DIVERSITY

Although the size, scale and scope of *Rogue One* will feel like a tentpole movie, Kennedy points out that "the interesting idea inherent in what we're trying to do with the stand-alone films is we're not trying to lock ourselves into something that's really specific. There's a huge opportunity to do smaller, slightly grittier films as well as films that get close to the size and scale of the saga films. We're trying to have a wide diversity."

In the making of the original legacy *Star Wars* saga films, George Lucas was very influenced by many genres of filmmaking, including everything from John Ford westerns to Akira Kurosawa films to World War II movies. "That's the wonderful thing about the stand-alone films," says Kennedy. "We're looking at these different genres and different directors with their own styles of storytelling. So, it gives us a very wide range and huge palette of opportunity."

When it came to finding the right story to lead off the stand-alone series, Kennedy found it in her backyard. As luck would have it, one person who had been secretly harboring an idea of his own was Industrial Light & Magic chief creative officer and senior visual effects supervisor John Knoll. Having been at ILM for nearly 30 years and as visual effects supervisor on several of the *Star Wars* saga films—*The Phantom Menace, Attack of the Clones,* and *Revenge of the Sith*—Knoll is almost unequalled in his knowledge and passion for the films.

But, it was this opening crawl from *A New Hope* that really fired his imagination:

Episode IV
A NEW HOPE

It is a period of civil war. Rebel spaceships, striking from a hidden base, have won their first victory against the evil Galactic Empire. During the battle, Rebel spies managed to steal secret plans to the Empire's ultimate weapon, the DEATH STAR, an armored space

1 / Donnie Yen on set. 2 / Veteran *Star Wars* actor Warwick Davis.

3 /

4 /

station with enough power to destroy an entire planet. Pursued by the Empire's sinister agents, Princess Leia races home aboard her starship, custodian of the stolen plans that can save her people and restore freedom to the galaxy…

Who were these rebel spies and how did they manage to steal the secret plans to the Empire's ultimate weapon? Armed with these simple questions, Knoll began to formulate an idea based on the events. And then the opportunity came to take his story idea one step further.

THE PITCH

"I'd known Kathy for about 20 years," says Knoll, "but it was still quite a unique experience to go up to the office of the president of Lucasfilm and pitch a story idea. I did about a seven-page treatment and went up to the office and pitched it to Kathy and Kiri Hart [Senior Vice President of Development]. I thought at least I'd done the pitch so I wouldn't always wonder, *What if?*"

Fortunately for Knoll and for *Star Wars* fans everywhere, both Kennedy and Hart shared his conviction, and a week later Knoll received an e-mail saying they were "seriously thinking of putting my idea into production."

Kennedy says, "I've known John for many years and worked with

> **"**
> ## The story was so compelling that I immediately knew this could be great.
> **"**

him as a visual effects supervisor, and I knew how talented he was and how much he cared about *Star Wars*. It was the first time I'd been in a situation where someone had pitched a *Star Wars* idea. I didn't know what to expect.

The story was so compelling that I immediately knew this could be great. And, lo and behold, it's become the first stand-alone movie we're doing."

In addition to the films that inspired George Lucas, films such as *The Dam Busters* and *The Guns of Navarone* proved inspirational to Knoll, and together he, Hart and the story team began to flesh out the idea of a film set in a time of extreme conflict with the Empire—a time of impending war.

"This is a time after Episode III and the purge of the Jedi where all the remaining Jedi have gone into hiding," Knoll explains. "It's before Obi-Wan comes back and Yoda reappears. Ordinary citizens are the ones who have to step up and show their heroism."

The "ordinary citizens" in this case turn out to be Jyn Erso and a band of unlikely rebels thrown together by circumstance who find themselves faced with the impossible task of finding the architect of the Death Star and stealing the plans. ▶

3 / Hyperspace re-created in the comfort of the studio! 4 / Director Gareth Edwards kicks back with the stormtroopers on set.

5 /

6 /

7 /

8 /

EVERYDAY HEROES

The end result is a story of hope and determination played out on a huge canvas but retaining the intimacy of a small film. It showcases the efforts of everyday people from very different walks of life who choose to do extraordinary things for the common good.

From the genesis of the stand-alone series idea, Lucasfilm felt it was important to the look and feel of these films that the chosen directors be empowered to tell the stories in their own ways. As Kennedy says, "What really sets the stand-alone films apart are the genres we are exploring, the unique stories we are telling, and the types of directors we are choosing."

When their search led them to Gareth Edwards, whose unique shooting style utilizes intimate, handheld camera work, they knew they had found the director they wanted for *Rogue One*. "We were really excited when we met Gareth Edwards," Kennedy says. "He had been on our radar for a long time, starting with the release of his first film, *Monsters* (2010). When he made *Godzilla* (2014) we knew that he'd taken the next step in big, tentpole moviemaking."

Explaining Edwards' fit for *Rogue One*, Kennedy says, "Gareth has that wonderful combination that is uniquely suited to *Star Wars* films, which is an emotional

> "
> ## Knowing these films could be different was exciting.
> "

understanding of the characters inside the *Star Wars* universe, and a sense of what is a strong family-type film that appeals to all ages. Gareth has a unique ability to combine a sense of humor with thematic storytelling."

A UNIQUE IDENTITY

Rogue One is an action-adventure story in the genre of World War II movies, and as Kennedy says, "Gareth Edwards is bringing an authentic feel to the movie that is very different from any other *Star Wars* film. He is telling an intimate father/daughter story set on a huge canvas."

Once he signed on, Gareth Edwards knew that before he could focus on the important job of casting the film, he had to take a step back and think how he could give the film its own identity within the *Star Wars* universe and make it his own.

"We're the first one out, so knowing these films could be different was exciting, but how different was the big question and what does that mean," says the director. "I love *Star Wars*. I grew up with the original trilogy and to me they're the ultimate movies. I feel that a massive upside to not being a part of the saga is we have a license to be different. And hopefully we took that license and ran with it."

Edwards continues, "We're going for realism and naturalness to the environments and performances ▶

5 / Filming the battle scenes that would bring an all-new reality to *Star Wars* combat. 6 / Preparing a death trooper. 7 / The crew shoot a scene with Jiang Wen (Baze Malbus). 8 / Gareth Edwards in action.

ROGUE ONE: MISSION DEBRIEF | 11

9 /

and characters we meet. It's also that we're part of the original films in terms of where our characters are. It had to marry to the films I grew up with. And there's a classical style to those, which is very considered and stable. We were also excited about doing something that felt more real and immediate."

HANDS-ON

Kathleen Kennedy was very supportive of Edwards' desire to experiment and to give the film its own unique personality. "Gareth is a filmmaker who appreciates the hands-on process of making a movie," the producer says. "He wants that camera on his shoulder; he wants to see the image; he wants to have that connection with his actors. I think that is very much a part of his process, so this handheld feel, up close, inside the action, is something that's really important to him and it came across in the footage that we were seeing."

Edwards wanted to give *Rogue One* a sense of gritty realism very reminiscent of his style of filming in *Monsters.* "What I wanted to do

was to make *Rogue One* more natural, more realistic and a little more organic; to make it feel like a real world. This is a time with no Jedi, no god to come and help the people who are under this massive threat," the director explains.

Striking the balance between that which is familiar to fans and taking the universe in a new direction led Edwards to award-winning cinematographer Greig Fraser, famed for his work on *Zero Dark Thirty* (2012) and *Foxcatcher* (2014).

For Edwards, Fraser turned out to be the perfect choice. "We had similar tastes," the director says. "What he loved about cinema I loved. It was a great relationship where we egged each other on, encouraging each other. We tried to set a really high bar. We surrounded ourselves with images and photographs we thought were the best, and even had a rule that we'd not watch anything other than our favorite masterpiece movies in the months beforehand. We wanted to feel every film out there was brilliant. And, so, we had a lot to compete with."

Edwards and Fraser soon discovered that they shared more than the same taste in films—they had a mutual love of operating the camera themselves. They also shared the same unusual approach to filmmaking, which is to light the background not the actors.

Edwards expands: "We're not trying to light the actors; we're lighting the environments so that the actors can go where they want and we'll find the cinematic beauty in it. We're giving them freedom, and it's inspiring as every day you get something you weren't expecting, and that's exciting as it gives you something unique."

In order to create the look and feel they wanted for *Rogue One,* Edwards and Fraser went back to the camera lenses of the 1970s and combined these with modern digital technology. Lucasfilm also has a history of breaking new technological ground, and the unique combination of these period lenses, with their cinematic feel and epic quality almost countering the cleanness and crispness of digital filmmaking, once again does just that. ●

9 / Producer of *Rogue One* and Lucasfilm president Kathleen Kennedy and producer Allison Shearmur talks with Diego Luna and Riz Ahmed on set.

ENCOUNTER

ON LAH/MU

In a quiet corner of the Outer Rim, a tale is set in motion
that will have enormous repercussions for the galaxy.

The remote world of Lah'mu is the setting for the prologue to *Rogue One: A Star Wars Story*. It introduces Mads Mikkelsen as Galen Erso, Jyn's father and a brilliant scientist. One of the galaxy's most renowned polymaths, Galen is a gifted theoretician, mathematician, and experimental physicist who is being pursued to complete a top secret research project for the Empire under the watchful eye of Director Krennic.

Mads Mikkelsen "Krennic is a man of power who is convinced that there is one solution to the problem that the entire galaxy is facing. And that solution happens to be the project he needs Galen's expertise to deliver. Galen is caught up not only in his work but in Krennic's ambitions as well."

Kathleen Kennedy "Galen is somebody who we want to feel compassion for, but we're conflicted because he's working for the Empire. I think that's the beauty of having somebody like Mads. He's such an extraordinary actor, and you completely believe that his commitment is a moral commitment."

Mads Mikkelsen "It's a big honor to be part of this legendary film ▶

1 /

1 / Orson Krennic arrives on Lah'Mu in search of his old friend, Galen Erso.

2 / A death trooper finds evidence of further members of the Erso family.

3 / Death troopers leaving destruction in their wake.

"

Whereas stormtrooper costumes are made for anyone over five foot nine, death troopers are over six feet tall.

"

universe. Something that is very interesting to me about *Star Wars* is that it's quite human, even though we have droids and different kinds of creatures that look very different from the human race."

To create the look of Galen Erso, director Gareth Edwards asked artists Neil Crossman and Glyn Dillon to look at *A New Hope* and the character of Luke when audiences first meet him while he is working on his uncle's farm.

Glyn Dillon "We first meet Galen at the very beginning of the film and Gareth wanted him to feel like

this was a cool *Star Wars* land. He wanted everyone seeing the film to immediately feel that they are in a *Star Wars* film that they love and they know. So Gareth said, 'Look at Luke's costume and do a darker version of that.'"

David Crossman "It's similar from the point of view of farming and the homestead and the *Star Wars* mythology. So, in the end, Mads ended up with a silhouette similar to Luke's but with a quilted crossover jacket in darker tones, as we didn't want to replicate it exactly."

In addition to the stormtrooper, Edwards also wanted to give fans

something new and terrifying, and so the death troopers were born. The death troopers are a completely new design specially created for *Rogue One*. They are an elite group of fighters who accompany Krennic wherever he goes. Whereas stormtrooper costumes were made for anyone over five foot nine, death troopers are over six feet tall.

Glyn Dillon "They're much taller and skinnier, and the costumes much tighter than the regular stormtrooper. Gareth wanted them to have a real sense of fear, and as they are entirely black, their silhouette is really intimidating." ●

4 /

5 /

4 / Luke Skywalker's costume as seen in *A New Hope*. 5 / Luke's costume provided inspiration for Galen Erso's attire.
6/ A death trooper stands amidst the carnage of Lah'Mu.

THE HIDDEN FORTRESS

ꓶꟽƐꓦꚸ ꓘꓵ1ꓘꓵꟽ

BASE ONE YAVIN 4

Away from the oppresive gaze of the Imperials lies the Rebel Alliance's secret base, inside the Massassi Temple on the moon Yavin 4.

The familiar rebel base on Yavin 4 from *A New Hope* appears in *Rogue One*. For budgetary reasons, George Lucas was only able to build a part of the rebel base, relying on a matte painting to give the illusion of size. The *Rogue One* production team was able to go all-out on its construction. Furthermore, the team was able to revisit the exact location of the original Yavin 4 set: Cardington Airfield in the county of Bedfordshire.

Cardington Airfield was originally a facility for building airships with a history dating back to 1915. The enormous 800-foot-long hangars offered concept designer Doug Chiang, senior art director Al Bullock, and co-production designer Neil Lamont the opportunity to build Yavin 4 to scale.

Neil Lamont "We have actually been able to build a set of enormous proportions. At the front you see it as a massive temple with a long aperture, which is the entrance to the Yavin hangar, and then inside the set measures about 350 feet in length by 200 feet in width."

Doug Chiang "You really get the sense of a fully operational hangar once inside. There are various crew and creatures rushing around mobilizing against the Empire, and we had enough space to feature full-size X-wings."

Al Bullock "In the middle of the huge hangar, we built the bunker set, adding a ceiling to make it feel a little more intimate."

Taking center stage in the bunker is the Yavin briefing table—a table painstakingly re-created by Academy Award–nominated set decorator Lee Sandales. The table first appears in *A New Hope* but unfortunately there were no drawings or blueprints to assist with the re-creation. So Lee and art director Lydia Fry had to resort to a detailed study of photography and film footage.

Lee Sandales "We set about doing a forensic study of the table, down to millimeters. It took about four to six weeks of drawings to get the table right. We used production photos of Carrie Fisher standing next to the table to get the height and to work out the scaling of the ribs on the inside of the table and also to work out how many ribs there were.

"We couldn't work out the graphics for the screens behind the table, so Lydia forensically went through working out each of the graphics so they exactly match *A New Hope*."

In addition to the X-wings, the film welcomes the U-wing into the rebel fleet.

Doug Chiang "Gareth is such a huge *Star Wars* fan that he wanted to design a ship as iconic as the X-wing. He wanted to create a Huey helicopter version of an X-wing so it had all the design and iconic features, but that could carry 12 people."

Gareth Edwards "The look of the vehicle had to be perfect, and thus the design of the new U-wing took months and about 1,000 separate designs to get right."

Doug Chiang "We had to get it just right. We needed a ship that would stand next to the X-wing."

Mon Mothma, played by Genevieve O'Reilly, is facing a time of dissent within the Rebel Alliance. Although unified in their fear and loathing of the Empire's aggressive expansion, the rebel leaders differ greatly in their belief as to a as to a solution. Many think they should continue to negotiate, whereas others believe direct action is the only hope for peace.

Genevieve O'Reilly "Jyn and Cassian have come back from a very important mission and with information about the brutality of the Death Star. It's a very low point in morale. Mon Mothma is very defeated by the Empire, but she believes in hope and she believes in Jyn. She sees the fight in her."

Returning to the role he first played in *Revenge of the Sith* is Jimmy Smits as Bail Organa. The senator from Alderaan has a daring plan to restore hope to the galaxy.

Jimmy Smits "One of the key themes in *Star Wars* is how we achieve our goals in a political situation and there are a lot of parallels with the world today. Sometimes the best intentions get lost because of the vying back and forth between countries and factions, in this case planets and galaxies. Bail is a politician but he also tries to be a man of action."

Observant fans will notice the change in Bail Organa's look. Reflecting his desire to act rather than attempt to placate the Empire, Organa is seen in more of a military role than in the prequels, with a khaki costume replacing the regal purple hues.

A new hero emerges amidst tragedy and possible personal betrayal: Jyn Erso, played by Felicity Jones.

Gareth Edwards "We talked about the fact that Jyn isn't just a woman—she's a person. We always tried to treat her like that. I wanted to make a character that I would want to be. Not to fancy her or want to marry her, but want to be her. It was just a cool person. We tried to make the film in such a way where the issue of boy or girl never came into it."

Kathleen Kennedy "*The Force Awakens* and *Rogue One* having

1 / Jyn Erso: rebel prisoner.

2 / Mon Mothma: rebel leader.

3 / The rebel base on Yavin 4.

4 / General Davits Draven plans his next move.

1 /

2 /

3 /

4 /

5 /

strong female characters is very indicative of what we're talking about doing going forward. We are finding diversity in our cast, whether it be ethnic diversity or male/female, representing the population. We need to make sure that the diversity in our society is reflected in the stories that we tell."

Felicity Jones "The thing about Jyn is that everyone should relate to her. It doesn't matter whether she's female or male. She's not just tough; like all human beings she can also be vulnerable.

"At the beginning of the film, she's very much a maverick. She's her own person. She's someone who naturally doesn't know how to keep to the rules and is always pushing the boundaries.

"I wanted Jyn to be as human as possible. She's strong when she needs to be, she's incredibly determined and she has to be tough when she doesn't feel it. Gareth has made everything feel as real as possible. He wants authenticity and that's hard work with harsh conditions, continual rain, sand being kicked in your face, but he wants an audience to feel that they are actually there and that's so important."

6 /

Kathleen Kennedy "Felicity is such a brilliant actress and brings a sense of gravitas and importance to everything she does, yet there's a real whimsy to her, too. She has a great smile, a wonderful sense of humor, and she's been fantastic. She shows the strength and empowerment that we're looking for in female characters in *Star Wars*. One day I hope we don't even have to talk about that because it will just be accepted that the female leads in *Star Wars* are as important as their male counterparts and recognized beyond gender for playing a great role."

7 /

5 / Jyn suggests her daring plan to the Rebel Alliance.

6 / Rebel captain Cassian Andor.

7 / Rebel commander Admiral Raddus.

8 / Jyn interrogated by rebel command.

9 / An astromech performs his duties on the base.

8 /

9 /

To create the soldier look of Jyn Erso, costume designers David Crossman and Glyn Dillon worked closely with Felicity Jones over the course of several months.

Felicity Jones "The costume was one of my favorite parts of Jyn. We looked at a lot of different references. We liked Japanese influences, so Jyn's undershirt was based on a Japanese design.

"It was important that Jyn had a toughness and strength but rooted in femininity. We didn't want her to be just dressing like a guy. She needed her own identity and her own way of doing things that came through her clothes."

Crossman and Dillon decided upon one main look for Jyn, a military look that could be pared back as the story progressed.

David Crossman "She starts off laden in Special Forces gear, but we continually strip this back to reveal her more human side, so by the end of the film you get a simple silhouette."

Glyn Dillon "She's got just the one main look but we also added a 'concho' for the Eadu mountain mission, which we named because it's like a coat mixed with a poncho. The only other look is the disguise she wears on the

Imperial landing pad. This is a really cool outfit with an Imperial gunner's helmet with a movable visor and underbite."

A rebel soldier with a checkered past, Cassian Andor, played by Diego Luna, is a man haunted by his past missions.

Diego Luna "The film has many layers. There are moments that are deep and dramatic and deserve a lot of attention and rigor as actors. Then there are scenes that are just fun and it's like choreography. You're enjoying and having fun with the beat."

10 / Jyn on the bustling rebel base.

11 / A rebellion from the Rebellion! Cassian Andor and a squad of soldiers prepare to disobey their leaders and head to Scarif.

11 /

Kathleen Kennedy "You sense that Cassian has had trouble with the Empire in the past. He clearly has lost family members, so he's damaged in some way. He's following orders initially when he meets Jyn, but as the story progresses, they both discover that they have a lot more in common than they realized."

Gareth Edwards "When Cassian and Jyn first meet, neither of them wants to be doing what they're doing together. Cassian would rather do it on his own, and so would Jyn. They initially don't get along too well but they're both likable people. That antagonism can't last too long because these two are going to solve this massive problem in the world of our film."

Felicity Jones "Jyn is suspicious of Cassian. She's put in this position of going on a mission with someone she's never met before in her life. She's naturally cautious about him. They're both similar in that they're both headstrong. They're not immediately best friends, which is fun to play. But they go through so much together. They can't help but create this bond. There's a true friendship, and true respect, by the end of the film. They really earn each other's affection."

In creating the look of Cassian Andor, Glyn Dillon and David Crossman looked closely at the influence of military costumes through the ages and, of course, at the *Star Wars* films themselves. David Crossman "Cassian starts out as a regular rebel intelligence officer, so we've given him the classic jacket with striped sleeves with his rank. Then we thought it would be cool to add a parka for the Eadu mountain mission, which was influenced by the one Han Solo wore in *The Empire Strikes Back*."

Glyn Dillon "He has the classic *Star Wars* shirt that flaps open like the one Luke wore in *Return of the Jedi*. And at the end of the film, like Jyn, we see him disguised as an Imperial officer."

Diego Luna "Buttons aren't allowed in *Star Wars*. You don't think about it, but then no one has a button. How do you attach stuff? It's a mystery."

Alan Tudyk plays K-2SO, a reprogrammed Imperial security droid now loyal to the Alliance. Tudyk brings his sense of comedic timing and presence to the task of bringing the droid to life via motion capture. ▶

12 /

14 /

13 /

15 /

> "
> # Having a member of your team who is a droid is a plus because they can do things that humans can't.
> "

Gareth Edwards "Alan is like all great comic actors in that, as funny as he is, he can pull at your heartstrings as well. We didn't want K-2 just to be the comic relief. There is something slightly tragic about him trying to find his place in the world. There are moments of fun, but Alan gives him a soul.

"K-2 was built by the Empire, but Cassian reprogrammed him. He had a memory wipe, but it wasn't totally effective so now he's more childlike and says socially inappropriate or offensive things without realizing. He's like a child and speaks his mind."

K-2 belongs to Cassian and, although it takes a while for Jyn to trust a droid that was once the property of the Empire, he eventually becomes an invaluable member of their small rebel team.

John Knoll "The idea for K-2 was that in the *Star Wars* universe, your small group of experts with complementary skills could extend to physical diversity. So having a member of your team who is a droid is a plus because they can do things that humans can't."

Alan Tudyk "He doesn't think of himself as owned. He and Cassian are a team and that allows for a lot of humor."

Simon Emanuel, production manager "Alan is an incredible comic actor. He is naturally incredibly funny, and he knows CGI, so he knows he can throw in lines and they can take whatever they want. And Alan takes it seriously. He wants to know about the character—the way it looks, the way it moves—and shapes his performance with that in mind."

Felicity Jones "Alan is so brilliant. He's improvising all the time, throwing in different lines to crack us all up."

The creation of K-2SO took the combined skills of Knoll and the team at ILM, and Neal Scanlan and his team of creature and droid experts. K-2 was first created as a full-scale maquette by Scanlan's team and then realized by visual effects.

Neal Scanlan "Gareth described K-2 as like a lazy sprinter; he's quick and incredibly powerful, and it's almost as if he doesn't class himself in the same bracket as other droids. The Empire version of a droid would be something you could take into battle. So, he's tall, very stealth-like and has long limbs to cover ground. Luke Fisher was the designer, and we made a full-scale model, which then became a visual effect.

"Robotic limbs have developed amazingly and allowed us to make Alan much taller. His leg extensions were built specifically for him, as were his hand extensions with robotic hands. So as an actor he can live out the scene and be as strong as the other cast."

Alan Tudyk "I have mechanical hands to make K-2's hands work. His hands are much longer than my own. They're animatronic. They can even grip things. I have one scene where I grab a guy by the shoulder, bring him over to another droid, and tell it that he's a spy and to process him. And, I just use my hands. They have a little power to them. They're very lightweight and are hollowed out. Everything was considered." ●

12 / Starfighter Command, General Antoc Merrick.

13 / Brave Blue Squadron pilot Vangos Grek (Blue Six).

14 / Rebel technicians prepare for a daring mission.

15 / An X-wing fighter, the most distinctive ship in the rebel arsenal.

CITY UNDER SIEGE
JEDHA

The peaceful Holy City of Jedha, crushed under the
weight of Imperial occupation, is the location for
a devastating attack by the Empire.

1 /

For the inspiration behind the creation of the Holy City of Jedha, production designers Neil Lamont and Doug Chiang, and supervising art director Al Bullock, looked to the ancient city of Jerusalem and the desert fortress of Masada in Israel.

Neil Lamont "One of the special things about *Star Wars* is that, even though we're creating new universes, it's still very much grounded in reality. Doug and I started with a lot of research and looked at real locations. In the case of Jedha, it's a very ancient city, but with little bits of tech to turn it into *Star Wars*."

Doug Chiang "George Lucas, who is a real history buff, would tell people when he started *Star Wars* to go back into history to find different elements, then take things that are from disparate times and merge them together. What you get is a design that is timeless, but seems very real because 80 to 90 percent of it is real."

Another key influence in the creation of Jedha was occupied Paris in World War II.

Al Bullock "Jedha is a holy city but occupied by the Empire and policed by stormtroopers. These are peaceful pilgrims held at gunpoint until finally they fight back."

The 'battle' in Jedha involved major preparation by Neil Corbould and his special effects team, with around 500 to 600 'bullets' exploding in the walls. Neil Corbould "Gareth wanted to film it almost like a documentary, like *The Hurt Locker* (2008) or *Black Hawk Down* (2001) with handheld cameras within the firefight so you actually feel as if you're there."

During this fight, the stormtroopers drive straight through the middle of the streets, scattering the innocent pilgrims. For this, Corbould sourced a tractor tank, which could spin on the spot.

Neil Corbould "We made one side in fiberglass and the other in a biscuit-foam material, so that when we blew it up it wouldn't hurt anybody."

Bodhi Rook, played by Riz Ahmed, is a cargo pilot who works for the Empire, but changes sides when faced with a harsh truth. ▶

1 / The once peaceful Holy City of Jedha.

2 / An ominous Star Destroyer.

3 / Imperial stormtroopers maintain order on the streets of Jedha.

4 / Defecting Imperial pilot Bodhi Rook on a mission to find Saw Gerrera.

2 /

3 /

4 /

" Subconciously throughout the film,
Jyn is putting together a team. "

Riz Ahmed "Gareth described Bodhi as a guy in a war movie who isn't supposed to be there. Everyone on the team is a soldier or warrior in some way and there's this guy who is there by accident but realizes he has to step up and make himself valuable. He's an everyman, someone audiences can relate to."

Felicity Jones "Subconsciously throughout the film, Jyn is putting together a team, and when she comes across Bodhi she doesn't realize straight away that there is a connection between them. Jyn is very empathetic and doesn't like to see anyone suffering, so she instinctively wants to help him and that is the start of their bond and friendship."

Kathleen Kennedy "Riz is an extraordinary actor. He's an interesting character in this story—a bit like Rick Blaine in *Casablanca* (1942). He goes wherever he wants; he doesn't really choose his side and it doesn't really bother him if he's working for the bad guys or the

good guys. In our story, he finds himself in a moral dilemma where he eventually does need to choose sides. Getting there and making that choice is what makes it interesting to watch him. Riz is one of those actors who also has this incredible ability to be funny and whimsical and yet extremely serious and dramatic at the same time. He's a very emotional actor to watch."

Riz Ahmed "I spoke to Gareth on the phone and he asked me to put something on tape for [the audition], so I sent him about 500 takes of one little scene. I was so excited!"

When it came to a look for Bodhi, Edwards initially envisioned him wearing glasses, but this developed into Bodhi wearing goggles.

Glyn Dillon "Bodhi wears a boilersuit with a sort of battle harness vest, giving him a look reminiscent of Dennis Hopper in *Apocalypse Now* (1979)."

Riz Ahmed "The costume is interesting because Bodhi is someone who starts off working for the Empire, then defects. But he never changes his clothes. He never puts on rebel clothes. That partly speaks to the action-packed nature of this film. There's no time for wardrobe changes."
Chirrut Îmwe is the blind monk whom Jyn first encounters when she and Cassian arrive in Jedha. But although without sight,

Chirrut is anything but unseeing. He is a skilled and artful warrior who can see into the hearts of all those around. And who better to play the role than martial arts expert and one of Asia's most popular actors, Donnie Yen.

Allison Shearmur, producer "Donnie Yen has so much wisdom, like his character, and he's got great humor. He has a sense of artistry and performance that tells us so much about his character. There's an elegance, a heroism, a nobility about both Yen and Chirrut."

In a time when the Force is all but forgotten and the few remaining Jedi are in hiding, Chirrut is a lone voice who still believes.

Donnie Yen "Chirrut is a true believer in the Force, and he preaches this.
"Throughout the whole film, he encourages and motivates his team members to have faith and continue to believe in the Force."

For the look of Chirrut, Gareth Edwards wanted him to be a skilled bowman, wielding a range of impressive weaponry, including a crossbow that more resembles a rifle in its capabilities and a cane that becomes a weapon when needed.
Chirrut's weaponry is concealed beneath his samurai-influenced robe, which can be thrown back when in battle, and completing the outfit are blue contact lenses with small holes giving Yen limited vision. ▶

5 / Riz Ahmed as Bodhi Rook.

6 / Donnie Yen as Chirrut Îmwe.

7 / Jiang Wen as Baze Malbus.

8 / Forest Whitaker as Saw Gerrera.

▶ Donnie Yen "We decided that the lenses would be blue. It's something different, and contrasts with the black hair."

Chirrut is not alone on Jedha when he meets Jyn and Cassian. He is with his faithful and longstanding friend, Baze Malbus.

Baze Malbus, a pragmatic soldier and a crack shot, has grown up with Chirrut and will follow his closest friend to the ends of the universe. Jiang Wen, one of China's biggest stars, was the perfect choice to play Baze.

Jiang Wen "Baze loves Chirrut, he believes him, he trusts him. They have a very close relationship from when they were kids, so even though they are very different personalities there is a real bond there and Baze will do anything for him. And Chirrut's friends are his friends."

Allison Shearmur "Jiang Wen is like Clint Eastwood; there is solidarity, a moral, a code, which may be corrupt but he absolutely believes in it. There is great chemistry between Donnie and Jiang, and a wonderfully warm humor. Theirs is one of the strongest fraternal bonds you'll see in the *Star Wars* history."

To create the look of Baze, Crossman and Dillon took "their favorite *Star Wars* elements like the partial armor and the boilersuit," a look which was then completed with a giant arsenal involving an enormous gun and backpack of ammunition.

Hair designer Lisa Tomblin gave what Jiang Wen describes as "a Bob Marley haircut," which was topped off by makeup designer Amanda Knight and her

9 /

9 / Baze and Chirrut in captivity!

10 / Imperial troops in action on the streets of Jedha.

11 / Blind fury! The troopers feel the force of a true believer!

team with "a very dirty face," befitting a soldier who is never off guard.

Saw Gerrera, portrayed by Forest Whitaker, is perhaps the most complicated character in this story and certainly unlike any other we have seen in the *Star Wars* universe before. Saw is an outlaw rebel, a man who believes that the Empire must be defeated, but at what cost? Is it acceptable to sacrifice the innocent for the greater good or does that make him as guilty as those he opposes?

Forest Whitaker "Saw is very clear about what he believes. It's the clarity of what he believes to be the solution to win the war before his world, as he knows it, is destroyed that makes others think of him as an extremist. He crosses lines, human rights lines.

He's willing to do things he thinks are necessary in order to save the people and to free them from the bondage and slavery of the Empire."

It is Saw Gerrera who rescues Jyn and subsequently raises her as his own daughter. However, Saw is a lone figure in the rebel fight against the Empire, a man who has rejected the Rebel Alliance, believing them to be ineffectual, and who has chosen to launch his own campaign against the Empire. Saw's methods are ruthless and he will not hesitate to kill the innocent for what he believes to be the greater good.

Kathleen Kennedy "He is kind of the moral center of the story, and casting somebody like Forest Whitaker was hands down Gareth's only choice, right from ▶

10 /

11 /

the beginning. The interesting thing about Saw Gerrera is that he came to the Rebellion early on as he was an activist who believed in the Rebellion. He was anxious to see the Rebellion come together and fight for what was right, and when we meet him in our story he's pretty disillusioned. It hasn't really come together in the way that he thought it would.

"Saw is the one who ultimately empowers Jyn. So he becomes a very important figure, not only to the story that we're telling, but most importantly to her because most everybody recognizes that it takes a mentor to recognize your strength and skills and give you courage to do brave things."

Felicity Jones "Saw Gerrera is the closest person that Jyn has to a parental figure. Not having her parents around, she's had to learn to be very self-reliant, and Saw Gerrera has shown her that not only does she have to rely on herself but she has to have strong convictions as well and defend those convictions. When Jyn and Saw meet, there's an incredible connection between them, a closeness and a bond. But, also, there's friction. You can see Jyn is trying to forge her own way.

"Forest is so brilliant technically, but also the most soulful human being I've ever met in my entire life. He brought such humanity to the character and such complexity. I feel speechless talking about him. I had a fantastic time with him."

In designing the look for Saw Gerrera, it was important to Gareth Edwards that Saw have nobility about him, almost as if he were a fallen king refusing to ▶

12 / Jyn hides out on the streets of Jedha.

▶ accept defeat, and this gave costume designers Glyn Dillon and David Crossman an interesting challenge.

David Crossman "Saw felt like a war-weary vet. We started talking with Gareth about him in terms of him being a king, an old king. So we tried to do a version of a medieval suit of armor with a flag on the back, as if a cape, and a guard over his shoulder, which gives him that silhouette of a fading king. But, underneath it's still a *Star Wars* space suit."

Saw's army consists of some of the strangest creatures yet seen in the *Star Wars* movies. Moroff and Bor Gullet are among the menagerie.

Neal Scanlan "There haven't been many versions of big, furry characters other than Chewbacca,

13 / Captain Cassian Andor on Jedha.

14 / Moroff: one of Saw Gerrera's loyal soldiers.

15 / Bodhi Rook in Saw Gerrera's lair.

16 / Edrio Two Tubes, Saw Gerrera's right-hand man.

and so we thought what can we introduce that would live alongside a Wookiee?

"Gareth liked the idea that this is a new breed of alien; characters that are a bit put-upon because they are powerful and can do a lot of lifting. Moroff is a bit disgruntled about his life but would never cross the line. So Ian Whyte, who plays him, used that as an understanding of how Moroff might move. He's a little bit lazy, as if he feels he really shouldn't be doing this all the time, but he's a good guy, so he's there to support."

Bor Gullet is Gerrera's henchman, a merciless interrogator who can read the minds of prisoners with or without their cooperation.

Perhaps Neal Scanlan's biggest and proudest achievement is the creature that literally broke the

mold, or at least records of the mold. The design for Bor Gullet resulted in Scanlan's team sculpting him at full size, something never before attempted, and this involved a staggering two and a half tons of silicone.

Neal Scanlan "Bor Gullet was a home run as far as character design. Normally there are many drawings and designs, but Ivan Manzella drew this blobulous, octopus-type thing and Gareth immediately responded 'that's it.' Bor has this incredible mind but is hampered by body, so we used that design as inspiration. He's a bit like Jabba the Hutt."

Gullet measured about 10 feet in length by 6 feet in width and the same again in height. It took 15 puppeteers to operate Bor, moving his body, tentacles and eyes, and making him breathe. ●

14 /

5 /

16 /

ᐅᑕᐳᐃᕋ ᕕᑕᐳᐱᐅ

A
NIGHTMARE
ON
MUSTAFAR

There are some corners of the universe that hold the
most terrible secrets. One such place is the lava-coated world
of Mustafar, home to Darth Vader.

Darth Vader
recuperates in his
bacta tank. Concept
art by Luke Fisher.

The task of re-creating the most famous movie villain of all time sounds easier said than done. After all, Darth Vader is one of the most recognizable figures in contemporary film history across the globe. However, for costume designers Glyn Dillon and David Crossman, the task wasn't as straightforward as one would first imagine.

Glyn Dillon "There's more than one look for Vader in the original films because in each film, his helmet or something on him would change. The fans will know there are the *New Hope* helmets and the *Empire Strikes Back* helmets, and they're slightly different."

As it turns out, the helmet worn by Vader in *The Empire Strikes Back* is shinier than its predecessor, but after much discussion Edwards decided that he preferred the less shiny version as first appears in *A New Hope.*

David Crossman "There are also differences in the neck cowl, and if you look closely at Vader's face in *A New Hope* you will see a slight C-shaped scar. So, we've kept the scar and tidied up the pipes a bit on his face.

"The rest of the costume is quite a faithful reproduction with the boxes on Vader's belt matching exactly those in *A New Hope*, even down to the little scratches. And the chest box is again painted wood with buttons on it." ●

AMBUSH ON EADU

The inhospitable, rain-soaked world of Eadu is secretly the location of the facility where Galen Erso and his team of scientists are reluctantly working on the Death Star.

Having fled the crumbling ruin that was Jedha, Jyn and the rebels head off to the cold, wet mountains of Eadu. This environment couldn't be more of a contrast to the dry desert lands of the Holy City, but it presented a whole new challenge to the art directors, Doug Chiang and Neil Lamont.

Doug Chiang "Gareth really liked the idea of a secret base, almost hidden. So we built a set that we then needed to find a way to hide. It's a dark, mysterious planet, constantly raining, and, in fact, always enshrouded in mist, which helped to cloud the design." ▶

1 /

2 /

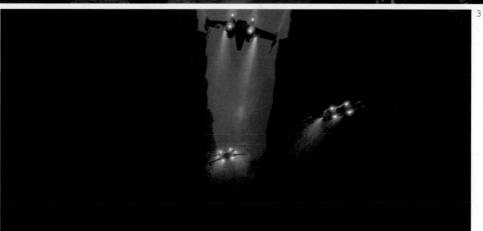

1 / Imperial officers and death troopers signal the arrival of Director Krennic.

2 / Cassian Andor prepares to take a shot.

3 / The rebels arrive to save the day?

4 / K-2SO pilots a U-wing through hostile skies.

▶ **Neil Lamont** "The biggest challenge was how to achieve a set of this size within a stage. Normally, something this big you would build outside, but with the continuous rain needed over a ten-day period of shooting, the effects, explosions, et cetera, it was easier to control on a stage."

The art department thus decided to build the set in an enormous purpose-built tank on the Richard Attenborough stage at Pinewood. And with the painted backing and the special effects department throwing continual wind and rain at the cast, it is easy to imagine that they were experiencing the very inhospitable weather of Eadu. ☻

5 /

6 /

5 / The team make a swift escape from Eadu.

6 / Cassian Andor: a man on a mission.

7 / Jyn fights on the stormy world of Eadu.

7 /

8 / The team
reflects on the
tragic aftermath
of the mission
on Eadu.

IMPERIAL POWER

THE DEATH STAR

The Empire is poised to unleash
its ultimate weapon on the galaxy.
Can Orson Krennic be stopped?

1 /

One set that needs very little introduction is the Death Star. However, for art director Alex Baily, who was charged with its re-creation, there was very little information to go on.

Alex Baily "We figured out the size from working out the size of one wall panel and just going from photographs. The original set was just cobbled together, and they only built the screen and one wall. Then when the day came to film on it, George Lucas decided he couldn't cover the scene with such a small set and so over lunch they built the rest of it!"

After weeks of careful research and forensic examination of photographs, Bailey and the team re-created the full set measuring 58 feet in width by 21 feet in height.

One change to how the set originally looked was the use of a giant LED display screen. Rear projection was used in *A New Hope,* and the filmmakers on *Rogue One* were planning to use blue screen, but at the 11th hour discovered the existence of a state-of-the-art LED display. This meant that the visual effects team could provide live, in-camera footage to run outside the iconic Death Star window while the cameras were turning.

Orson Krennic, played by Ben Mendelsohn, is the man behind the creation of the Death Star, a weapon he knows will allow the Empire to take full control of the galaxy through fear. Mendelsohn signed on to play the malevolent character.

Kathleen Kennedy "Ben Mendelsohn was one of the first people Gareth started talking about for Krennic. He's unsettling if he chooses to be and at the same time there's a childlike quality about him that makes you feel that he could easily start laughing at any moment."

"Consequently, given the fact that we have Darth Vader in this ▶

1 / Orson Krennic, flanked by his death troopers.

2 / The director weighs his next move.

2 /

3 /

4 /

▶ movie, finding a villain who could be juxtaposed against Darth Vader was a real challenge, and I think Ben has done an incredible job acting alongside one of the most iconic villains ever to be in movies."

Ben Mendelsohn "When you've got Darth Vader on the playing field, no one is taking his spot. He is one of the greatest villains of all time; no one's going to top Darth so you can relax and do what you need to do."

"Krennic believes in the Empire very thoroughly. He sees it as a way of maintaining order and that the Empire is essentially correct in what it does. But he is someone from the outer colonies, a guy who has worked his way up. He's not officer class, but he's gotten to

5 /

where he is because he's driven and can just do it, and he knows that."

Glyn Dillon, costume designer "There's a character in the Death Star in *A New Hope*, blink and you'll miss him, but he was later named Yularen. He is wearing a white tunic, and so we thought it was a great look for a villain."

David Crossman, costume designer "We found out that these were supposed to be intelligence officers. When the script came in and Krennic was described as an intelligence officer, we thought it would be great to put him in this white tunic. It would be the perfect contrast to Vader."

Completing the look is Krennic's

3 / A stormtrooper as seen in *Rogue One*.

4 / The Empire's finest as seen in *Star Wars: A New Hope*.

5 / The Death Star rains down destruction on the Holy City of Jedha.

pistol. Krennic is the only character in the film to carry a pistol.

Ben Mendelsohn "I figured the pistol has likely been passed down through generations. It's a powerful three-shooter. But Krennic doesn't draw it very often; he doesn't need to."

Stormtroopers are among *Star Wars*'s most iconic images, and the only challenge with re-creating something such as the stormtroopers exactly as they were nearly 40 years ago is whether it will stand up to modern-day digital technology. And that is why Gareth Edwards gave the direction to his creative team to "do it as you remember it, not how it was."

David Crossman "If you look closely at the original stormtroopers you will see they used stickers for detail. That wouldn't work today. So, we've made the helmets and costumes as fans remember them but we've used three-dimensional vents and detail."

Glyn Dillon "When we redid the stormtrooper helmet we made and sculpted it in a computer, but based it on a scan of the original. And then we noticed the helmet had quite a big squint because originally they were made out of clay and you're not going to get it perfectly symmetrical. So we tidied it up a bit on the computer, but still kept that slight squint as we wanted to honor that organic feel." 🔴

SKIRMISH ON
SCARIF

The final struggle to retrieve the Death
Star plans takes place on and above the
beautiful but corrupted world of Scarif.

"
Obviously we couldn't go to the Maldives and blow it up!
"

Jyn's search for the Death Star plans finally takes her and her rebel team to the beatific planet of Scarif. Art directors Neil Lamont and Doug Chiang were faced with an unusual challenge: re-create the beautiful Maldives beach in England!

Neil Lamont "Gareth had always wanted this area to be a beautiful place—a desert island with blue emerald water—so we have the contract of the Empire ruining something idyllic in order to make something destructive."

Doug Chiang "Gareth wanted to set up the third act in paradise, where the Empire is there to mine and strip the planet, to destroy it. He visualized somewhere like the Maldives, but obviously we couldn't go to the Maldives and blow it up!"

Having looked at beaches and locations as far-flung as South Africa, the filmmakers finally decided to bring the Maldives to England and found the perfect spot—Bovingdon Airfield, an old RAF base unused for nearly half a century, ideal for the purpose of re-creating the Maldives with its clear horizons and accessibility. All it needed was a bit of sand and some palm trees.

Neil Lamont "We shipped in 2,000 tons of sand in about 200 truckloads, and imported over 60 palm trees from Spain and various greenery from the U.K. We also needed to build a beach and the special effects team had the great idea of recycling water from the tank at Pinewood so it wouldn't be wasted."

In fact, the art department recycled 800,000 liters of water, about 5,000 baths full, into a giant tank measuring 200 feet by 100 feet. All told, the final set measured a staggering 700 feet by 500 feet, or about eight acres, and perfectly mirrored the locale of the Maldives where a small unit would later film.

The sequence features some all-new alien creatures joining the battle: Pao and Bistan.

Pao, a amphibious creature with a hinged mouth of gigantic proportions, was one of the first creatures designed for the film that Gareth Edwards really responded to. Creature effects supervisor Neal Scanlan worked on bringing Pao to life.

Neal Scanlan "Pao has very tiny eyes which he squints through and he spends most of the time with his mouth shut, but when he opens it, when he screams in battle, his mouth opens to an extraordinary extent."

When you look into Pao's throat, you see right down inside the performer Derek Arnold's throat. When performing Pao, Arnold was rendered almost blind and relied on choreographer Paul Kasey, who looked after the characters on set, and drove Arnold through an earpiece.

Neal Scanlan "A lot of the time Pao was running, ducking and diving amongst explosions on set and it was a challenge as he totally had to trust in the directions he's been given. Then there was a third person, Phil Woodvine, performing the physical expressions on Pao's face using radio-controlled animatronics." ▶

1 /

2 /

3 /

1 / An elite
shoretrooper.

2 / Members of Rogue
One prepare for battle.

3 / Baze Malbus
in action!

4 / Rebel warrior
Bistan.

5 / Pao on Scarif.

4 /

5 /

▶ Bistan was another design immediately favored by Gareth Edwards, who was amused by the play on the idea of putting an actual monkey in a space suit. Scanlan believes the attraction of Bistan, performed by Nick Kellington, lies in the fact that it's actually Kellington's own eyes fronting the character..

Neal Scanlan "It's Nick's eyes we see, not lenses. The reason I think Chewbacca works so well is that you actually see Chewie's eyes. It's a real person's eyes and that makes all the difference."

Much of the action of the third act takes place on the beautiful planet of Scarif, and thus at Bovingdon, including huge battles between the rebels and the Empire as Krennic endeavors to thwart their attempts to steal the Death Star plans.

As well as going through around 2,000 bullet hits a day, effects supervisor Neil Corbould's biggest challenge was to build an explosion of gigantic proportions as the Imperial shuttle, stolen by the rebels, is blown up. ▶

6 /

7 /

6 / Bodhi Rook plays his part in the assault on Scarif.

7 / Stormtroopers defend the installation.

8 / Baze Malbus brings superior firepower into the battle.

9 / Rebels take cover!

10 / The Empire scrambles to defend the installation.

11 / "I am with the Force, the Force is with me."

8 /

12 /

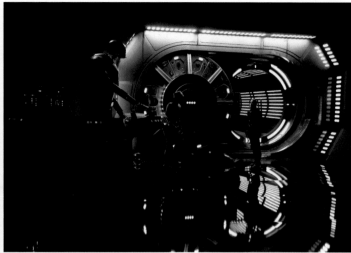

▶ **Neil Corbould** "Gareth wanted a big explosion, so we showed him some tests that were about a fifth of what the full explosion would look like. And so when we came to shoot it, we had a 40-foot container, which we basically cut into bits, loaded with mortar parts, and then we covered it in a lightweight breakaway material. I told Gareth it was going to be a bit bigger than he'd seen.

"Gareth wanted to get really close, and so I said it would be fine but he would have to dress up in a full fire Nomex suit, balaclava, gloves, et cetera. Everyone around him was also dressed up and wore fire suits, and we had stuntmen with shields around as well to protect him."

After three months of planning and testing, the special effects team finally had a day to rig the explosion, which was pre-rigged and then craned in. The final explosion could be seen for miles around as the 2,500 liters of fuel created a fireball about 200 feet high with a 50-to 60-foot radius.

The interior of the Imperial base on Scarif was filmed at a very unusual location—Canary Wharf tube station in East London. The towering modern platform perfectly mirrored the environment of the Empire, with its clean glass and chrome lines. But, due to the fear that the people passing by would notice, it had to be a fast build. Art director Alex Baily rose to the challenge.

Alex Baily "It was a very complicated logistical operation. We had no time to preinstall any elements. Everything had to be pre-built and constructed in one evening when the tubes had stopped running."

Having completed dry runs on Thursday and Friday nights, at the stroke of 1:00 a.m. on Sunday morning, when the tubes stopped running, the art department raced into action, laying a rubber floor, covering signage, adding greebles and graphics.

By 5:30 a.m. the unit wrapped and began to remove all traces of the set, so by the time commuters started arriving at 7:00 a.m., it was as if the production were never there. ●

12 / Krennic on the way to a final confrontation with Jyn Erso.

13 / The rebels on the cusp of completing their mission.

FILMING

The *Rogue One* production team was prepared to go the extra mile to capture the heat of battle.

CONFLICT

1 /

2 /

Attempting to tell the story of how a small band of rebels was able to steal the plans to the ultimate trophy in the Empire's war cabinet would mean a story involving conflict.

"There are war-movie elements in *Rogue One* and some moments that feel a little darker and grittier. I think we would be doing the concept of the movie a disservice is we suggested that getting the Death Star plans was an easy thing to do." says Kiri Hart, co-producer and senior vice president of development for Lucasfilm.

In order to achieve this sense of conflict and boots-on-the-ground, Gareth Edwards studied many historical war photographs. He shared this imagery with costume designers Dave Crossman and Glyn Dillon for ideas on the look of the costuming for the film.

In addition to costumes, Edwards' approach to creating an environment that would reflect the story he wanted to tell also applied to the art department and production designers Doug Chiang and Neil Lamont.

Chiang had first worked with George Lucas in 1995 on the prequels. "I remember George saying that for him *Star Wars* was a documentary, and that is what I loved and appreciated from Gareth's approach," Chiang says. "Gareth's style is very hands-on, very handheld, as if you are just coming into the world and just discovering the shots."

For Chiang and Lamont, "just discovering the shots" meant building 360-degree environments, knowing that wherever Edwards found his moment, they would be ready. "Working with Gareth is exciting as the camera has the potential to look anywhere on the set and our guys have to be ▶

4 /

5 /

3 /

1 / The Imperial army
fights off an insurgent
attack on Jedha.

2 / Death troopers man
the trenches on Scarif.

3 / Rogue One
prepares for war.

4 / The rebels create
a diversion.

5 / The war-torn
streets of Jedha.

6 / Shoretroopers
in battle!

7 /

8 /

ready with any wish that Gareth or Greig Fraser might come up with," says Lamont. "This means we had to cover every angle, which was a very exhilarating but rewarding challenge."

Lamont continues, "Ultimately what this is going to give you is a docu-war film, edgy and classy, a harder, rougher version, a tougher version than the *Star Wars* everybody is used to."

Equally, the challenge to make *Rogue One* feel grounded was welcomed by Academy Award–winning special effects supervisor Neil Corbould and his team.

Edwards charged Corbould with the task of making the action seem as real as any war footage. Corbould explains, "Gareth wanted a slightly more realistic look to all the battles, so rather than just a spark, you get lots of debris as well. We tried different materials giving different colored sparks, so if it was hitting metal, you'd get a blue spark and hitting earth would be a yellow-red orange.

"Our aim was that the characters would really look like they are in a battle, and that the danger was very real," he concludes.

10 /

11 /

7 / Death troopers hit the beach.

8 / Sergeant Melshi (Duncan Pow) looks for a target.

9 / Stormtroopers shoot at X-wings on Eadu

10 / Chirrut Îmwe prepares for combat.

11 / Chirrut Îmwe and his fallen foes.

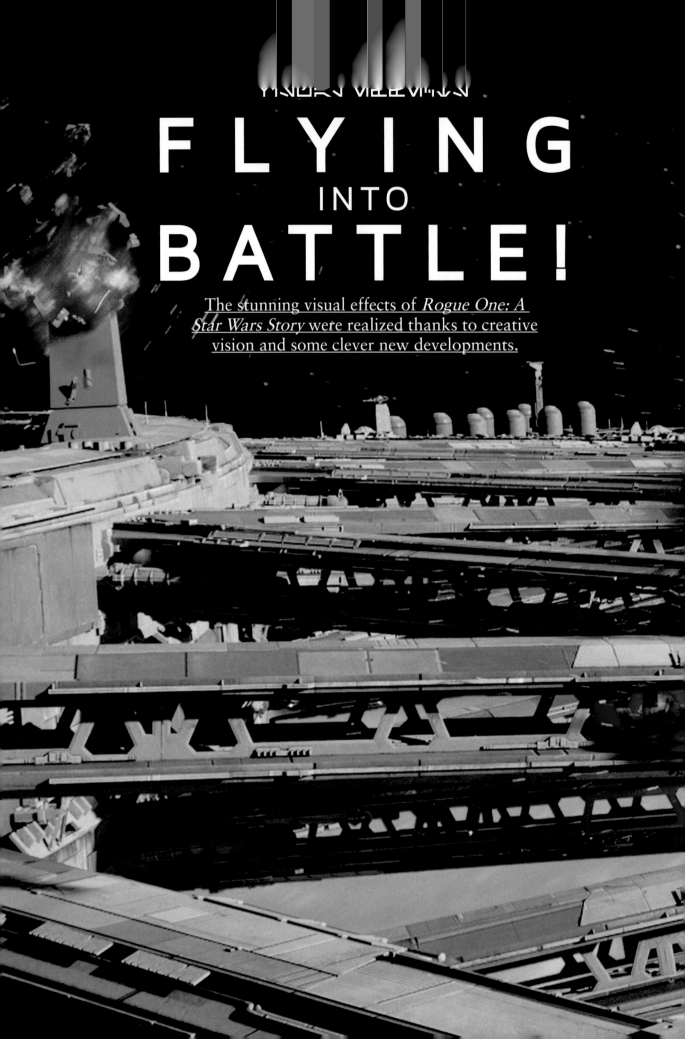

FLYING
INTO
BATTLE!

The stunning visual effects of *Rogue One: A Star Wars Story* were realized thanks to creative vision and some clever new developments.

> " The real-time visual effects would literally create the environment on the screen as the cast performed the scene. "

Being the world's leading authority on visual effects, John Knoll was able to introduce new and exciting technologies to the production of *Rogue One.*

Knoll brought real-time visual effects to the set, making it possible for Gareth Edwards to to gauge what the final world would look like while he was actually shooting the film. The real-time visual effects would literally create the environment on the screen for Edwards to watch as the cast performed the scene.

Describing the process, Knoll says, "SolidTrack is a technology that allows us to reach in real time where the camera is, then use that to drive computer graphic representation of what the part of the set is we don't have. It gives you a preview on the monitor of what the final result will be."

He continues, "Gareth had concerns about the use of green screen and I get it. Cinematographers train their whole life to light what's in front of them, so if you can see a preview of what that final image will be, you can make different choices."

Knoll also introduced new techniques when shooting the interiors of the ships as they battled through attacks by the Empire. Historically, although a craft may be placed on a gimbal to simulate movement, the

exterior would often be blue or green screen.

"One of the challenges is cockpit work, and we have X-wings, a U-wing and Empire shuttle cockpits," explains Knoll. "Traditionally you do these on sound stages and light it for daytime exterior. But we wanted to take this up a notch. So we've made this giant wraparound LED screen that's 50 feet in diameter with a central band 20 feet high, and we have imagery we play on these screens. By taking this approach we can add lasers that fly by in the space battle and you can see the reflections in the shiny surface of the helmet the pilot is wearing. And that creates a very real look."

The design of the ship belonging to Admiral Raddus also brought with it advances in the way visual effects can marry with production design to find solutions. Working closely with Neil Lamont and Doug Chiang in the art department, Knoll came up with the groundbreaking idea of building a 3D visual effects set that would be painted by computer in postproduction.

Knoll walks us through the idea. "There wasn't a big budget for something that was going to be on screen for less than 30 seconds, so we elected to do a virtual set. We stuck to the idea of building the basic forms of the set to cast shadows to provide the lighting ▶

1 /

2 /

3 /
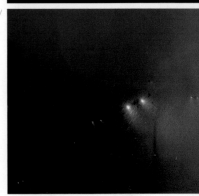

1 / A dazzling shot of an X-wing diving for the sheild gate high over Scarif.

2 / Blasting into hyperspace.

3 / Battle over Eadu.

4 / A view from the cockpit of an X-wing fighter.

5 / A U-wing in hyperspace.

"
We wanted to make a digital version of the model kit library.
"

6 /

6 / The attack on Scarif
featuring the rebels'
new ride, the U-wing.

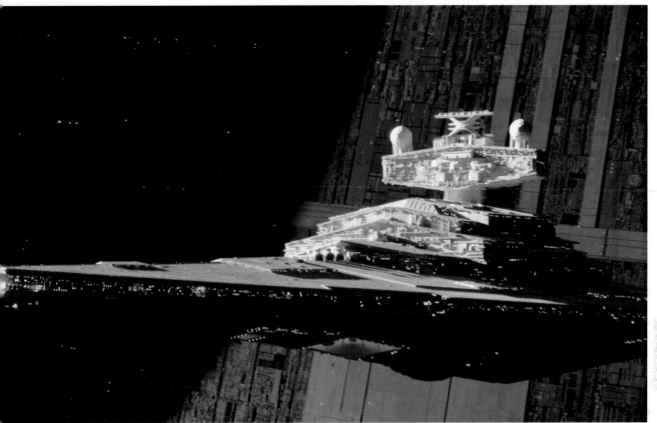

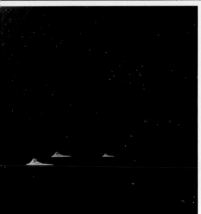

7 /

environment for Greig Fraser. The idea is that we then replace them with computer graphics. We haven't really done something like this before."

And finally, Knoll created a 21st century alternative to an art form created by Lucas and his team nearly 40 years previously. "An important part of the original *Star Wars* films was the way miniatures were built," says Knoll. "The *Millennium Falcon*, the Death Star and Star Destroyers were all made by 'kit bashing.'"

This simply involved breaking down multiple off-the-shelf plastic kits that were intended to produce small replicas of aircraft, ships and vehicles, and stripping these kits of their component parts, which would then be repurposed to create these phenomenally detailed models. The idea was simple, but the process took hours and hours, involving thousands of kit elements.

Knoll explains, "They used tiny pieces of model kits for artillery, tanks and race car engines and then fixed them onto a *Star Wars* model. Since we're going to be building a great many assets of various kinds, spaceships, et cetera, we wanted to make a digital version of the model kit library so we could take a similar process, and hopefully the aesthetic would be the same across the films." ◉

7 / Digital versions of the Star Destroyer and the dreaded Death Star re-created by John Knoll and his team.

STARDUST
MEMORIES

The cast and crew of *Rogue One: A Star Wars Story* share
their favorite childhood *Star Wars* memories.

A long time ago in a galaxy far, far away...

TWENTIETH CENTURY-FOX Presents
A LUCASFILM LTD. PRODUCTION
STAR WARS
Starring MARK HAMILL HARRISON FORD CARRIE FISHER
PETER CUSHING
and
ALEC GUINNESS
Written and Directed by GEORGE LUCAS Produced by GARY KURTZ Music by JOHN WILLIAMS
PANAVISION® PRINTS BY DE LUXE® TECHNICOLOR®

ONE SHEET –STYLE 'A'   77/21

GARETH EDWARDS

I was just two years old when *Star Wars* came out, so I don't remember seeing it in the cinema. But I do remember sitting in the back of a car after having a falling out with my parents. They went somewhere and came back with a box, and it was a Betamax player that played films! I remember instantly asking if we could get *Star Wars*. They were already ahead of me because my next-door neighbor had it on Betamax. We went round their house to borrow it, and I don't think I ever gave it back. We went home, put it in, and I felt like I knew what I was doing for the rest of my life: I'm watching this over and over on a loop. Every morning I'd put it in, eating breakfast, then I'd have to go to school.

I don't think I'm lying when I say *Star Wars* still means the world to me. My biggest regret is that someone didn't tell me when I was four that I was going to make a *Star Wars* film someday. I'd have spent the last 36 years planning it out.

RIZ AHMED

I was quite young when the first films came out. It was my older brother who was more into it and could follow the stories. For me, it was a series of incredible images I never forgot: the Ewoks, the AT-ATs, Jabba the Hutt, Han Solo being frozen in carbonite. All these images stayed with me and inspired me. And, very soon after seeing those films with my brother, we'd run around the house and create our own movie worlds. Then, we would write down the title after we acted them out.

KATHLEEN KENNEDY

Gareth Edwards went back to Tunisia, where the movies were shot. He drank blue milk. He posed in a way that Luke Skywalker did next to the hut on Tatooine with the two suns. He took a picture so he could remember what he felt like when he saw the movie for the first time.

The great thing about Gareth and the great thing about the filmmakers we're bringing in is they're all fans. They all have a deep emotional connection to *Star Wars*. That's something that's really important as we look around and identify the people who will direct these films. We're looking for caretakers—people who genuinely care and accept a responsibility around the franchise.

FELICITY JONES

I grew up with my older brother and lots of boy cousins. I remember them all sitting around watching it earnestly as I came in through the door. I remember that incredible title sequence from *A New Hope* going up the screen. But, I have to say, my affection for *Star Wars* came from watching it in preparation for *Rogue One* and going back to watch those early films and becoming rather obsessed with it.

DONNIE YEN

I saw the first *Star Wars* back in 1977. At the time I was living in Boston and, like everybody else, I was overwhelmed by *Star Wars*. Here it is years later and I never expected to be a part of *Star Wars*. It's an experience, and all these memories from when I was a teenager and saw *Star Wars* for the first time started rolling back.

FOREST WHITAKER

I've seen all the *Star Wars* films. I was really excited by them. I liked the concept of duality and the concept of what was the potentiality of a human being. What we're capable of when we tap into our own sense, our own Force, and see what we can do. It's very powerful. It explored not just the unknown, good and evil, dark and light, but potential—the potentiality of being a universal being, a human being.

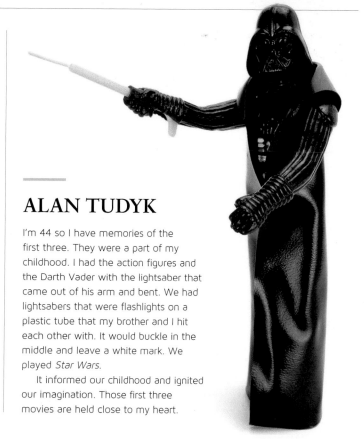

BEN MENDELSOHN

I loved everything about *Star Wars*. I still remember the bubble gum cards that you would get, and I still remember there was a card with Chewbacca and Han sort of like going, "pew-pew"! It was number 44 in the series. It was very hard to get, and I wound up getting two of them.

It took a lot of chewing gum, but I was very glad I got two. *Star Wars* was a very big deal.

ALAN TUDYK

I'm 44 so I have memories of the first three. They were a part of my childhood. I had the action figures and the Darth Vader with the lightsaber that came out of his arm and bent. We had lightsabers that were flashlights on a plastic tube that my brother and I hit each other with. It would buckle in the middle and leave a white mark. We played *Star Wars*.

It informed our childhood and ignited our imagination. Those first three movies are held close to my heart.

ROGUE ONE
A STAR WARS STORY

The story of Jyn Erso, her quest for the truth, and the events that restored hope

> "
> # They call it the Death Star. There's no better name. And the day is coming soon when it will be unleashed.
> "

1 /

2 /

As the Clone Wars raged across the galaxy, the Republic began construction on a moon-sized battle station, based on a Separatist design, in the hope of completing its construction before the Separatists potentially finished their own station. However, the Republic discovered that creating the primary weapon required a scientific leap forward.

Lieutenant Commander Orson Krennic offered to enlist one of the galaxy's most respected scientists, Galen Erso, a former university acquaintance, to provide the breakthrough.

IMPRISONED

Galen worked for Zerpen Industries on the planet Vallt, using crystals to generate energy, with the long-term goal of low-cost, renewable energy for the entire galaxy. A pacifist and a conscientious objector, Galen remained neutral, even as the war reached Vallt. Captured, alongside his pregnant wife, Lyra, they were taken prisoner by Separatist forces.

After months in prison, during which time Lyra gave birth to a daughter, Jyn, the Erso family was rescued as part of a daring Republic operation led by Orson Krennic. Before taking the family back to Coruscant, they visited Galen's home planet, Grange. Shocked to see his home so battle-torn, Galen questioned his neutrality.

Having arrived on Coruscant, Krennic and other members of the military tried to subtly persuade Galen to join their efforts on the battle station under construction in orbit around the planet Geonosis.

Cleared of suspected treason by Wilhuff Tarkin, at the instigation of Krennic, Galen was assigned a non-research position on the planet Lokori.

As the Clone Wars reached a sudden end, with the Separatist leadership killed and the Jedi Order eradicated, the Ersos relocated back to Coruscant, where Krennic had set up Project Celestial Power in order for Galen to continue his energy research using kyber crystals. While this was seemingly to provide power sources to Imperial worlds, it was, in fact, a cover for the construction of the battle station's weapon. ▶

3 /

1 / Jyn Erso, rebel insurgent and key player in the search for Galen Erso.

2 / Director Orson Krennic, the man charged with completing the Death Star.

3 / Krennic and his squad of death troopers.

4 /

5 /

6 /

▶ A SECRET FACILITY

Krennic hired the smuggler Has Obitt to leave decommissioned weapons on the planets Samovar and Wadi Raffa as a ruse for the Empire to eventually occupy these worlds.

Krennic had set up a satellite facility on the planet Malpaz without Galen's knowledge, where the scientist's former colleague Dagio Belcoze inadvertently killed thousands in an attempt to test the energy output. The deaths were attributed to anarchist elements opposing the Empire.

4 / Cassian Andor covers his tracks on the Ring of Kafrene.

5 / Touchdown on Scarif as the battle begins.

6 / Cassian, K-2SO, and Jyn in disguise.

7 / Jyn Erso: prisoner!

8 / Underground spy Tivik informs Cassian Andor of the Empire's evil plans.

Krennic became suspicious of Lyra's influence on Galen and plotted for her to lead a survey team to Alpinn. On completing the survey, Obitt showed Lyra and fellow surveyor Nari Sable the planets Samovar and Wadi Raffa— the protected worlds ravaged by the Empire's mining efforts.

Lyra returned to Coruscant to find her husband entrenched in his work, and the Celestial project under increased security. Galen was growing suspicious about the use of his research. He continued to make breakthroughs, learning

how to use the kyber crystals to amplify energy beams. Krennic had a Star Destroyer equipped with a twin laser array, which was successfully tested.

Obitt was dispatched on another mission, this time to the Salient system. With the help of Saw Gerrera, he covertly arranged to warn those in the system of the Empire's intentions.

THE TRUTH

Tarkin demanded access to Salient, but unlike Samovar and Wadi Raffa, the system ▶

7 /

8 /

10 /

9 /

11 /

12 /

9 / Jyn Erso on the rain-soaked world of Eadu.

10 / Rebel extremist Saw Gerrera in his stronghold on Jedha.

11 / Bodhi Rook, the defector who brings a message of hope from Galen Erso.

12 / The streets of Jedha: the first casualty of the Death Star.

▶ fought back, destroying facilities used for the Imperial machine.

The grand moff suspected that Krennic had allowed Obitt to warn the Salient system in an attempt to further his career.

Krennic's research team, oblivious to the true purpose of their research, were killed by Krennic. Returning to Coruscant, he discovered more evidence of suspicious behaviour by Galen and Lyra. He threatened her with prosecution, resulting in Lyra and Galen discussing their extreme reservations about the project.

After the Salient system was finally subjugated, Obitt was captured. Under interrogation by Tarkin the smuggler confessed his traitorous actions.

The Ersos confronted Krennic on Coruscant. He learned that Obitt's ship was coming to Coruscant. In the belief that Obitt was helping the Ersos to escape, he ordered their detention, but it was too late. Obitt had arranged for Saw Gerrera to liberate the Ersos, taking them away from their Coruscant "prison."

ROGUE ONE

After much searching, Krennic found Galen Erso on the remote world of Lah'Mu. Killing Lyra, the ruthless director took Galen while his daughter Jyn went into hiding. She was eventually rescued by an old family friend, Saw Gerrera.

Thirteen years later, Bodhi Rook, a defecting Imperial pilot, delivered a holographic message from Galen to the rebel faction hidden on Jedha led by Saw Gerrera.

JYN'S STORY

Jyn Erso, freed from Imperial captivity by the rebel forces, was recruited to find her father.

After Jyn joined forces with rebel captain Cassian Andor and his reprogrammed Imperial droid K-2SO, they arrived at the Holy City of Jedha, where insurgents were uprising against the Empire's occupation. With the aid of two former Guardians of the Whills, blind warrior Chirrut Îmwe and mercenary Baze Malbus, Jyn found her old revolutionary mentor Saw Gerrera. He showed her her father's message, in which he spoke of his love for her and revealed the true circumstances of his involvement on the project. Galen also revealed that he had included a tiny yet devastating vulnerability in the Death Star's reactor that could be used to destroy it. He informed Jyn that the structural plans could be found at an Imperial installation on Scarif.

Aboard the Death Star, grand moff Tarkin expressed skepticism about the project and Krennic's management of it. The director focused the weapon on Jedha's capital and fired. Jyn and her team fled, with Bodhi Rook in tow, as Gerrera was killed in the blast. Despite the success of the test, Tarkin announced his intention to take control of the project.

Finally tracing her father to an Imperial research facility on the storm-lashed world of Eadu, Jyn was forced to offer him a bittersweet goodbye after he was killed in a rebel bombing raid.

Unable to verify Jyn's story, the Rebellion did not know what to do next. Jyn, Cassian, ▶

13 /

16 /

▶ K-2SO, and a number of rebel soldiers hijacked a stolen Imperial ship to steal the plans themselves. Using the callsign "Rogue One," they left the rebel base on an unauthorized mission.

Krennic arrived to personally review Galen's communications to discover what information had been disclosed. As Jyn, Cassian, and K-2SO searched for the design plans, the small group of soldiers enagaged the garrison of stormtroopers. Supported by the hastily scrambled rebel fleet, which had arrived to attack the shield gate that controlled access to the planet, the battle raged on.

As Jyn obtained the schematics from the data vault, K-2SO was destroyed fending off stormtroopers. Rook, Îmwe, Malbus, and several other rebels all fell in the battle. As Krennic confronted Jyn, he was shot by Andor.

High above the battlefield, Tarkin elected to use the Death Star to destroy the compromised base. As Jyn used the base communication system to send the Death Star schematics to the rebel command ship, the weapon was fired. Krennic, Jyn, and Andor were later killed as the base was obliterated.

As the rebel fleet attempted to jump into hyperspace, an Imperial Star Destroyer commanded by Darth Vader intercepted and boarded the command ship. Despite Vader's efforts, the schematics were passed onto a Blockade Runner and into the hands of Princess Leia Organa as she raced to deliver the plans to a mysterious Jedi general named Ben Kenobi… ✪

Star Wars: Catalyst: A Rogue One Novel by James Luceno and *Rogue One: A Star Wars Story* are published by Del Rey books.

14 /

13 / The rebels infiltrate the base on Scarif.

14 / Imperial troops scramble to repel the rebel assault.

15/ The Dark Lord of the Sith, Darth Vader.

16 / Orson Krennic looks on as the rebel forces attack Scarif.

17 / Jyn Erson, disguised as an Imperial gunner, on Scarif.

15 /

17 /

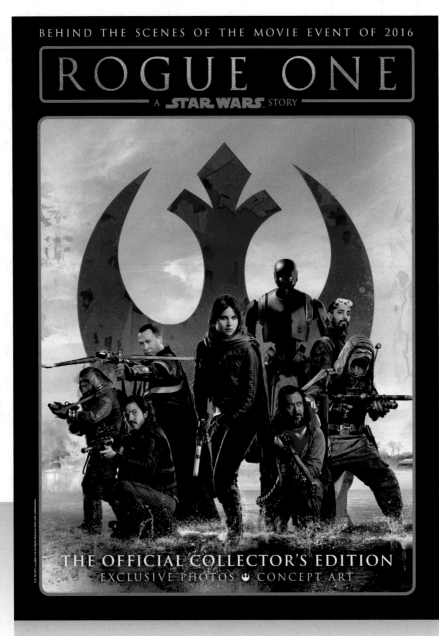